STRICTLY NO CROCS

by Heather Pindar

Illustrated by Susan Batori

Zebra invited everyone to her party **except** of course...

...The crocs.

"Let's sneak into the party and eat everyone up!" said Cruncher.

"Yes, but how?" said Chomper.

"Don't worry," said Snapper.

"I have a clever plan..."

So one by one, the **crocodiles** sneaked into **Zebra's** party.

First **Cruncher**...

then **Chomper**...

First **Cruncher** tried to jump as high as the **Springbok** on the bouncy castle.

BOING!

BOING!

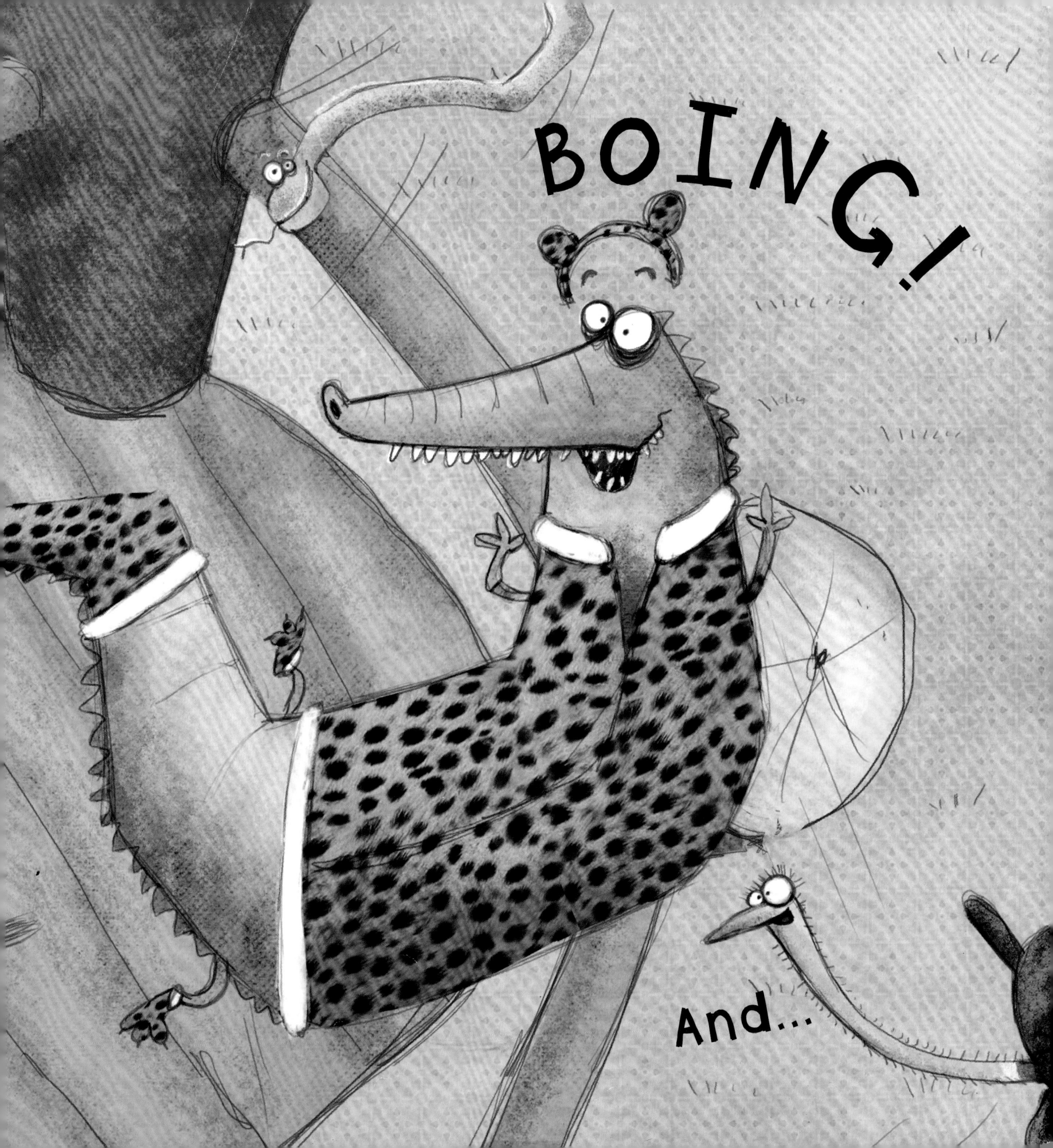

...Chomper played pass-the-parcel.

"I've won a **teddy bear!**" he yelled.

He could hear everyone singing.

HAPPY BIRTHDAY TO YOU

Then out came the **cake!** Zebra blew out the candles.

Snapper ate so much cake he got **stomach ache!**

Next everyone danced the **conga**.

The crocs led the way singing...

"**Na-na** **na** **na**

"Hurray!"

Down came the balloons.

BANG!

BANG!

BANG!

Everyone burst
as many
balloons
as they
could.

Later...

...They went out into the garden.

FIZZZZZZ!

BANG!

OOOOOOOH!

"Fireworks are my favourite!" sighed Chomper.

All too soon the **party** was over and

Cruncher,

Chomper

and Snapper

were saying their **thank yous** and waving **goodbye**.

They started the **long** walk home.

"**Wow!** What an **amazing** party!" said Chomper.

"**Fantastic!**" agreed Cruncher.

WE

TO EAT

EVERY

FORGOT

BODY

UP!

"Never mind," sniggered Cruncher.

"It's Giraffe's birthday party next week..."

The End

Strictly No Crocs
An original concept by author Heather Pindar
© Heather Pindar

Illustrations by Susan Batori
Susan is represented by Good Illustration
www.goodillustration.com

Published by MAVERICK ARTS PUBLISHING LTD
Studio 3a, City Business Centre, 6 Brighton Road,
Horsham, West Sussex, RH13 5BB, +44 (0) 1403 256941
© Maverick Arts Publishing Limited January 2016

A CIP catalogue record for this book is available at the British Library.

ISBN: 978-1-84886-187-9

www.maverickbooks.co.uk